1 MONTH OF
FREE
READING

at

www.ForgottenBooks.com

By purchasing this book you are eligible for one month membership to ForgottenBooks.com, giving you unlimited access to our entire collection of over 1,000,000 titles via our web site and mobile apps.

To claim your free month visit:

www.forgottenbooks.com/free88170

ISBN 978-0-331-00977-4
PIBN 10088170

Wampum and Old Gold

HERVEY ALLEN

NEW HAVEN · YALE UNIVERSITY PRESS
LONDON · HUMPHREY MILFORD · OXFORD UNIVERSITY PRESS
MDCCCCXXI

ACKNOWLEDGMENT.

FOR permission to reprint poems appearing in this volume, thanks are due to the editors of *The North American Review*, *The New Republic*, *Contemporary Verse*, *Life*, *La France*, *Harvey's Weekly*, *The Southern Review*, *The New York Times*, *The Boston Evening Transcript*.

" Though my hands have not learned to model
  The dreams of a groping mind,
Though my lips have not spoken their music
And are leaving no songs behind,
Think not that my life has been futile,
Nor grieve for an unsaid word,
For all that my lips might never sing
My singing heart has heard.

" I have etched the light on a willow
With neither a plate nor style;
I have made a song of the crescent moon
And a poem of only a smile;
Are they less because lips could not know them,
These songs that my heart has known?
Am I wholly mute who have sung with my heart
And sung with my heart alone?"

F. F. H.

CONTENTS.

POEMS WRITTEN SINCE 1918

CONFESSION.

I THINK, by God! It is no lie;
I shall go dreaming till I die!
There is no love so real to me
As the cold passion of the sea.
There is no little, wind-swept town
By harbors where the roads go down,
Or headland gray that sits and sips
The cup of ocean at its lips,
And gazes at the far-off ships—
Or tree or house or friend so real
As visions and the dreams I feel.

No—not the windy, vaultless arch
Where all the white stars flame and march,
Nor water at the river fords
Like horses mad among the swords,
Or oaks that lean from winter storms;
These only give my vision forms.

Away! White hands, I will not take!
And kissing mouths that cry, "Awake!"
For you I have no gramercy;
So leave me by my lotus tree,
To dream and gaze into the sky
Where red suns wither up and die,
I know! I know! I do not lie!
I shall go dreaming till I die!

DESPAIR.

You who made me
⠀⠀With first ecstasy
When I was sown,
And lovely things at night
I will not write
And burdened moan,
While veiny labyrinths with mystery ran
Till time and blood were life
And I began—
By holier things than God,
Or any other shibboleth of man,
Dead woman wan,
By the thin, silver scream that winter morn
In the dim, shuttered room where I was born,
Be gone!

Haunt me no more, Shroud Trailer,
Go to bed.
For the swift, golden wings I owe to you
Flap in the dust like some loose, common shoe;
Stay dead, stay dead!
I fear your glimmering bust in utter air,
The transparent eyes with shadowy stare,
The sleepy, sleepy scent of flowers
And the long hands—
They fill me with despair.

Touch me no more at night.
Borrow no form for me
Of sound or sight;
For all my days are spent by cluttered streams,
Distracted by a thousand things and faces,
And all unuttered die great dreams
Among the stagnant places.
I am not what you gave your life to buy,
And God knows what I shall be by and by!

14

The motes of habit sift down grain by grain,
Till I am what I am in heart and brain,
So young—so old—
Death keep you, darling,
Deaf and blind and cold.

VALE.

I LOVE the little vale between your breasts,
But yet, farewell, for that is never still;
My garden far from you will be at rest
With lakes asleep beside a brooding hill
And cedar swales in hollow valley lands
With S-like streams between the O-shaped ponds,
Where grow frail ferns with upturned Gothic hands
And prayerful fronds.

In gray half-lights 'twill be a lovely thing
By Gypsy paths to wander at hearts-ease
Near campaniles where the bell folk sing
Down terraces of rustling linden trees,
And two hills like your breasts will be in death,
When lamps will cast their shadows silently,
Will rise still blue above the yellow corn
That ripples with a sleepy mystery.

AFTERMATH.

UNDER the placid surface of the days
  So seeming clear,
Back of the habits of old ways,
A quiet fear;
The locked-up memories of war,
Our Bluebeard's room,
Where the blood creeps underneath the door.

Never will come
In streams of days that ring
Like clean coins down the merry grooves of change,
One without grief's alloy,
Struck from pure gold of joy,
Undimmed by unshed tears,
Nor is it strange.

For in the wraith-thronged brain
Are private ghosts of pain,
Aloof, like patient sick men in a crowd
With half-veiled faces and old sorrow bowed—
Ah! The free days can never come again!
They passed with the far, rolling drums,
Died to the moan and thunder of the guns,
And the mad, glad, clear, lyric birdsong never comes.

HYLAS.

Theocritus, Idyll XIII.

W HERE *art thou, Hylas,*
  Of the golden locks?
Where art thou, Argive lad,
That fed thy flocks
In wind-swept Thessaly,
Beside the sea?
Alas! Alas! for thee,
Hylas, Alas!

I.

When the Pleiads rose no more
Rowed the heroes to the shore,
Much in fear of winter gales,
And they furled the wing-like sails,
Carrying up the corded bales
From the hollow, oaken Argo
Till they lightened her of cargo.
Then they beached her for the winter
Where nor rocks nor waves could splinter
There the heroes made their camp
By the whispering seashore damp,
But the mighty Heracles,
Tired of looking at the seas,
Rose and left those sounding beaches
For the upland's wind-swept reaches.

In a little beechwood gray
Hylas fed his flock that day,
Playing all alone but gayly
Where he fed his lambkins daily,
Singing to a five-stringed psalter
By a little woodland altar,
Where a shepherd's fire of oak
Made a ribbon scarf of smoke,
Curling highly, thinly, bluely,
From the faggots cut but newly.

18

Moving with a god-like ease,
Through the gray boles of the trees,
Hylas first spied Heracles,
Looming vast as huge Orion,
Tawny in his skin of lion;
While through interspace of leaves,
Through the network autumn weaves,
Fell bronze sunshine and bronze leaves
On the lion skin with its paws,
Dangling, fringed with crescent claws.

Softly all the flock were bleating
As he gave the lad good greeting,
Rubbing down with leaves his club,
Mighty as a chariot hub—
Hylas stood with golden locks,
Glowing mid the lichened rocks,
Laughing in the silver beeches,
White as milk and tanned like peaches.
Then the hero loved the lad,
For his beauty made him glad,
And he took him on his knees;
Tender was huge Heracles,
Telling him of strange journeys
To the far Hesperides,
Crossing oceans in a bowl,
Till he won him heart and soul.

So these two were friends forever,
Never seen apart, together
Were they all that winter weather.
And the hero taught the youth
How to shoot and tell the truth,
How to drive a furrow straight,
Plowing, plowing, very early
When the frosty grass was curly—
Taught him how to play the lyre,
Till each wire, and wire, and wire
Sang together like a choir;

And at night young Hylas crept
In the lion skin where he slept
Where the lowing oxen team
Stood beneath the smoke-browned beam,
Slept beside the hero clypt
By the giant, downy lipped.

Centuries have fled away
Since the hero came that day
To the little beechwood gray
Where young Hylas was at play;
But I shall, as poets may,
Wreathe these roses for his head,
For his beauty is not dead.
And a voice has sung to me
Like a memory of the sea,
Sung this ancient threnody,
Like an autumn melody:
"Alas! Alas! for thee,
Hylas, Alas!"

II.

When the springtime came again
And the shepherd to his spen
Led his cloudy flock again,
When the awkward lambkins bounded
While the twin pipes whistling sounded,
And old Charon from his glen
Saw below the smoke of men
Curling thinly from the trees,
Then the heroes sought the seas.
Then the Argo left the shore,
For each eager warrior thought,
When the Pleiads rose once more,
Of the golden fleece he sought.

Hylas went with Heracles,
Dancing to the dancing seas,
And he stood high in the bow,

Golden by the carven prow,
Or he lay within the furls
With the sea damp on his curls.
But at home his mother wept
With her hair upon the floor,
By the hearth where he had slept,
For her woman's heart was sore,
Saying, "He is gone from me!
Gone across the sounding sea!
Ai! Ai! Woe is me!
Alas! Alas! for thee,
Hylas, Alas!"

With the soft, south wind to follow
All the day the sail was hollow,
While the marvelous Orpheus sang,
Till the water furrows rang—
Never man sang as he sang—
Never man has sung the same—
And the ship flew till they came
Where the olive trees are gaunt
By the winding Hellespont,
And the Cian oxen wear
Water-bright the bronze plowshare.

On a fallow meadow hollow,
Where the Cian cattle wallow,
There they landed two by two;
They the grass and rushes strew
For their bed,
Leaves and pointed flag stocks callow,
Foot and head.
And the evening coming on,
Heracles and Telamon
Set the supper fires upleaping
And the shadows swooping, sweeping
Overhead.
Meanwhile, Hylas with a vase
Wandered inland through the haze,

Hoping there to fill his bronze,
Girt about with goat-foot fauns,
Polishèd.
And around and twice around it,
Where an inwrought girdle bound it,
Fled the rout of chaste Diana,
Goddess led.

Inland in a cup-shaped vale
Willow swart and galingale
Grew with swallowwort and sparsely
Maidenhair and blooming parsley,
And the shallow's level glass
Mirrored back the yellow grass
Where the swallow dipped his wings,
Making rings on rings in rings.
There a nymph dance was afoot
Where the country people put
Cloth and oaten cakes and bread
For the water spirits dread—
Two and two and in and out,
Three and two, around about,
Hands around and then they vanished,
Leaving Hylas there astonished.

But at last he stooped to dip
And the eager water slipped,
Stuttering past the metal lip,
Choking like a sunk bell rung—
Suddenly white nymph hands clung
Cold as iron around his arm
Till he cried out in alarm.
Gave a little silver cry
And the swallow skimming nigh
Darted higher in the sky,
And the echo when he spoke—
Awoke.
Now the white hands tighter cling,
Now the funneled water ring

Fills and flows till in its glass
Nods again the nodding grass.
Alas! Alas! for thee,
Hylas, Alas!

Then it was that Heracles
For sweet Hylas ill at ease,
Left the heroes by the fire,
Strung his bowstring taut as wire,
Went to look for Hylas inland
Past a little rocky headland,
Rising higher ever higher
Till he found the cup-shaped dale,
Where he called without avail,
Shouting loudly, "Hylas, Hylas,"
Echo answered back, "Alas,"
Echo answered very slowly,
Speaking sorrowfully and lowly,
When he called the lad, "Hy-*las*,"
Hollow echo said, "Alas."

And he never found him more
On the hill or by the shore,
On the upland, on the downland,
Never found him where he lay
Down among the boulders gray,
Limp among the watery rocks,
Where the lily raised its chalice
And the dread nymphs combed his locks,
Pale Nycheia, April-eyed,
And white Eunice and Malis.
For his voice came down to these
Vague as April in the trees,
Filtered through the water clear
Far and faint yet strangely near,
Very thin—
And no echo could they hear
Only ripples' silver din
And the dull splash of an otter;
Echo cannot live in water.

23

But that echo comes to me
Down through half eternity
Crying out, "Alas—Alas!"
For all beauty that must pass
Like a picture from a glass—
When time breathes it is not there—
Bony hands and coffined hair!
Alas! Alas! Alas!

BACCHUS IS GONE.

Bacchus *is gone!*
I saw him leave the shore
Upon a moonless time,
And he is gone—is gone—
Forevermore.
I saw the satyrs and the bacchanals—
Bacchus is gone—is gone—
With smoking torches as at funerals
Light him across the sea at dawn.

I saw the whimpering pards
Where he had passed—
Bacchus is gone—is gone—
Sniff to the water's edge,
Where purple stained, his footprints led—
I heard the Goat-foot whisper in the hedge,
"Bacchus is dead—is dead,"
And go aghast,
Snapping the myrtle branches as he fled.

Bacchus is gone!
And with him dancing Folly—
Bacchus is dead—is dead—
Oh, Melancholy!

No! No! He is not dead; he has but fled
To kindlier lands he knew in days before
Men snatched the purple roses from his head.
He does but wanton by some liberal shore—
Sun kissed—
And wreathed with vine leaves as of old,
With spotted beasts and maidens by his car,
And sound of timbrels like a story told
Of youth and love and blood and wine and war.

TIGER LILIES.

THEY make me think of battlefields I saw
   Where butterflies with wings of sulphurous gold
Crawled on gray faces death had made obscene
That stared with stolid dolls' eyes from the mold.
They make me think of pools of wimpled slime,
Where lizards bask upon the quaking crust,
And crumbling walls where hairy spiders weave
And snakes lie coupling in the summer dust.

I think it must have been along the Nile
That first these speckled membranes burst the pod,
Before the boy-flat breasts of some half-cat
Half-man and beryl-eyed Egyptian god.
Or first they grew about forgotten tombs
The apes inherit in hot jungles where
Like xanthic suns through aquid shade of leaves
A spotted leopard's dilate pupils stare.

These were the mottled blossoms of Gomorrah,
Wreathed on beast-gods by priestly Sodomites,
By Baal fires when the talking timbrel's sound
Fell from Astarte's groves on full moon nights.
They suck a yellow venom from the sun
And mid their reedy stocks there comes and goes
The forked, black lightning of a serpent's tongue
That hisses as his slippery body flows.

Such lilies bloom beside the gates of hell
And poison honey festers in their pods,
Olid as tales of lust told long ago
About the wanton mother of the gods.
And I would plant them by the lichened tomb
Of that veiled queen who died of leprosy
With two red princes smothered in her womb;
Their roots would feed on her in secrecy.

THREE LANDSCAPE MOODS.

THE FIRST: YOUTH.

YOUTH is a vale afire with hollyhocks,
  Robbed by those greedy publicans the bees,
Where cuckoos call like fairy story clocks
And blue-jays holla in the apple trees.
No thunderheads come up with black despair
To dim its arching orchard's leafy sheen,
But clouds like ivory towers pile in air
And gothic woods stand, cloistered, cool and green.

It is a glade where earliest flowers grow,
Along the melting snowbanks in the spring,
The waxen-stemmed anemones first show,
And Madame Woodthrush preens her dainty wing.
White hyacinths like masts with flower spars
Stand in the woods and dot each bosky lawn,
Like distant sails or clusters of pale stars
Against an emerald sky at early dawn.

Cleft in life's hills, Youth is a sheltered swale
Where for a while we lie in indolence
And watch time's waterfall thin as a veil
That falls and hangs and smokes in long suspense,
And there a fountain spouts of purest joy
That feeds the fall, birds whistle on its brim,
Often I lay beside it when a boy
And saw the future mirrored vague and dim—

Heaven was there a strangely clouded page,
Two rivers on the plains met like a "Y,"
And blue as ghosts the mountains of old age
Rolled down the western sky.

THE SECOND: HIGH TIDE O' LIFE.

High Tide o' Life's a city by the sea,
By tide rips where the flood comes shouting in,
On straits that bring up ships with spicèd freights
And sails as scarlet as a woman's sin.
A mart where merchants chaffer on the docks
For pearls and feather work and jewel'd shoon,
And hurry off to feast when all the clocks
Strike anvil-tongued a thousand-noted noon.

High Tide o' Life's a city proudly vain,
With minarets from whence men can descry,
Like domes of giants' houses, chain on chain,
Death's arid mountains arabesque the sky.
And hoary uplands wave with tasseled corn,
And long sun pencils strike the hills, afar,
The walled towns smolder in the fire of morn
Like embers of a sullen, fallen star.

High Tide o' Life's an upland where no breath
Of frost has ever crept across the grass,
But days as idle as a shibboleth
Like golden coins are quickly spent. They pass
In hidden valleys fit for secret lust,
Where strange winged-sins like griffin-hippogryphs
Bask with their glittering scales in white-hot dust
Along a sunstruck face of basalt cliffs.

It is an isle in red, witch-haunted seas
Where lovers' nights, the jade-faced moon stands still,
Pouring an amber twilight through the trees,
Across the copper ocean and the hill.
High Tide o' Life's a plain laid easterly
In realms ruled over by some fabled *Djinn*
Where rivers blue as *lapis-lazuli*
Rush down to meet the flood tides roaring in.

THE THIRD: OLD AGE.

Old age is like a bleak plateau,
About—around—the dead leaves blow
In shouting, keening winter wind,
Below life's plains lie cloud bedimmed
Below.
In long gray lines the dead leaves go,
The stone blue shadows limn the snow,
The thwacking branches creak and mutter
In scarecrow desolation utter.
In scarecrow
Clothes the last leaves flutter
And in dry hollows rasp and putter
About the starved, old, carven faces,
Around the ancient burial places
   About, around, below.

That land is very old and lonely
Beneath—among—the cliffs its only
Hope is kindling firelight
Before the coming of the night,
Before
There are no travelers there
Left any more to come and share
The shelter from the ghost wolves' patter,
The helter-skelter, bony clatter
The helter-skelter
And the scatter
Of riven, driven souls that chatter
Beneath the cliffs, while in and out
Among them raves the death wolves' rout,
   Beneath, among, before.

And ever from each waning fire
Away—away—against desire
The death wolves snatch their struggling toll,
And snarl and harry down a soul,
And snarl

And harry down one other,
And then another and another,
To where Death sits, an idiot,
That stirs all things into a pot,
That stirs
Till everything is nought
Except the stirrer and the pot;
Beside eternities midriff,
Where time is bordered by a cliff,
With creaking bones and dismal whoop
He makes God's bitter charnel soup—
"Away," he cries, "or we shall quarrel,
Away, my wolves, for more and snarl
   Away! Away! and snarl."

THE HERMITAGE OF BELLS.

A DRAMA OF SOUND.

Dramatis Personae.

> The King.
> The Queen.
> The World.
> The Five Bells.
> The Earth.

Time: The Middle Ages.

Place: Lusitania.

I.

THE king has built a hermitage of bells
    Beyond the city walls upon a hill,
Save when the bells are ringing for the king,
His garden by the sea is forest still.
Set on a cape curved like a hunter's horn,
Rock terraced like the temples of Cathay,
It overlooks the town and fields of corn
And glimpses topsail-ships at break of day.
And there a deep spring flows called *Blanchefontaine*
That sings a deathlike monody of rest,
All night the sick moon totters on its alban waters—
It drips a sound like summer rain,
When the sun opens up his eye,
Until he stares like Cyclops from the west.
It slips through oak groves with an easy motion,
Twinkling like starlight from its shady source,
Three times it curves before it meets the ocean
Across the tide rip hoarse.

Farther up
The oak groves end abrupt,
But down that narrow valley
Like a darkened alley,
The water falls and calls
And seeps and leaps

31

And speaks by waterfalls;
Till the wanderer believes
There are voices in the leaves,
Whispering like thirsty lips,
Calling like muffled bells from misty ships,
Gurgling like pigeons from the eaves—
It is a demon din
Of subterranean voices old and thin,
An elfin carillon the water rings
As it sweeps on.
Halfway in that night
Of oak twilight,
Where the stream dashes down a verge,
The sound of ocean and of river merge.
And it is strange to see
The leaves whirl eerily,
When like an icy kiss,
Comes the long withering hiss
Of the tormented sea.

The king is melancholy mad, I guess,
To dwell in such a dim and rustling place,
Perhaps he has a sin beyond redress,
Perhaps he sees him visions of a face.
Some say it is a bell
Has lured him to the garden by a spell,
And that the spell is holy;
Holy or not, it's melancholy!
For when the queen rides to him from the town,
With two maids posting, one on either side,
Her face is veiled with black when she rides down—
Like mourners by a hearse her two maids ride—
Her face is veiled with black,
The reins hang slack;
Some say she weeps,
But who can tell?
Why should the queen weep when she hears a bell?

She stops by the gate blind-walled;
Mary! What called?
Did something die?
What answered back?
Did the queen shriek behind her veil of black?
Something said, "O," "O," "o"
With the voice of the queen's own woe!
Was it demon or echo?
It had an "O"-shaped mouth
And a voice like the wind in the south.
It mocked her like a child,
Each time less loud
And much more mild.

The king, I guess, has lost his wits;
It must be so!
All day he sits
Where mast-straight poplars grow,
Four here, four there, foursquare,
Like columns in a row,
Still as the shadow on a mountain,
And in the middle is a fountain,
Held by two marble boys,
Whence the water falls with a sleepy noise.
It is a madman's choice
To listen to that fountain's voice.
It must be so!

For never comes to that enchanted place
A sound but of the water, sea, and bells;
The shadows lie like tattered lace.
One mood is fixed there and forever,
Like a look on a dead man's face,
Like a week of summer weather,
I would that I might lay my head on such a bed,
Where dreams make spells—
So must the king think when he hears the bells.

II.

Once in his youth,
While his new ears could yet distinguish truth,
He heard a listless bell clang langorously,
A liquid, languid clamor,
The talking tone of iron struck by the hammer,
A sound that blew like smoke across the sea,
Low, slow and trembling dreamfully
From the high, horn-shaped cape;
For there a hermit lived
And tended the wild grape,
Where white, campaniform, small lilies teem,
And there he died beside his cell,
Lost in his dream of heaven and of hell;
And the bell was the voice of that old dream.
One Lusitanian summer, long ago,
Upon a hot and azure afternoon,
While the oars trailed
And with the tide they sailed,
And tenor zithers sang an ivory tune—
Along cerulean coasts,
With islands like blue ghosts,
Rang the lone hermit's bell,
"*Alone-lin-lang-alone,*"
Clear as a wounded angel's voice,
Soft as a death spell that old women croon—
The harbor gulf lay placid,
And in the west there hung a half a moon.

Never again in laughter or in tears,
Or in titantic days of crashing shields,
In triumphs with blue light upon the spears,
Or when he rivaled God upon his throne,
Never had the bell's voice died;
In all his purple, blood-bought pride
It seemed to toll for him an overtone.
After the battle with his veins' blood spent,
Disheartened by the metal light of day,
Between the crisscross threads that made his tent,

The fear of life came on him as he lay;
"Outside the world is garish," thought the king,
And then—and then he heard the lone bell ring
And saw the peace and green light of a wood;
It was a very vision of escape,
A high-walled garden on the crescent cape,
Fair as an evil thing but good.

The cape is luniform
Whereon the hermit's form
Lies bony white and still
Beside the chapel on the hill;
The long grass waves as if he breathes
At every breeze that weaves;
The birds have nests among old votive wreaths
And there the snake sheds in the rustling leaves.
There are faint flower sounds
Around, for spider hands have rung
The lily with its yellow clapper tongue,
All day the mists take shape
And the high hawks slant drifting down the cape—
By night the heavenly hunter leads his hounds,
Wandering the zodiacal bounds,
And all the white stars march,
Flaming in the unalterable arch,
While the wind swings the listless bell
That rings the hermit's knell—
Sleep well, sleep well!

III.

Three years the king has dwelt within a cell
That he might dream his garden first to build it well,
His ministers are black with wrath
And the stone floor is hollowed to a path,
But still he hears the bell,
A frozen sound clear as a cold, deep well.
The king is melancholy mad, I guess.
At nights
The tower windows flash with lights

And many an artisan
Comes after midnight with the garden's plan
Of walls and towers
And terraces and flowers,
And spreads them wondering upon the floor;
The queen comes seldom now and least
Of all the priest;
There is no priest alive
That can the king's soul shrive;
The dead hermit from his cell
Has lured him close to heaven with his bell,
A strange, a mad, a melancholy spell.

The master of campanology
Has cast four lovely voices for the king,
Four godlike metal throats that sing
In towers at the corners of the wall;
And all the garden hears them call,
Four miracles of tone,
Of sound that flows to nothingness
Like water lines upon a river stone.

Gracious as a good gift given freely,
Comes from each campanile
At each corner of the wall,
The keen voice of a bell,
"*Lan-up, lan-up*," they ring,
And call and call the king
With the voice of the old spell
That they inherit from the hermit's bell—
Five times as strong,—
The king must go ere long—
He has the key to the garden gates,
He only waits
In courtesy to say the queen farewell.

Alas! Alas! The king is mad!
The people throng to see him pass,
And he has heard a mass.

It was an eery thing to see
The king go merrily
And all the world forgo—
At dawn when little birds sing charmingly,
There was a ringing sound of horses' feet
And lovers in their upper rooms stopped clinging,
To hear go down the street
The minstrelsy
And little foolscap bells a-ringing.

IV.

Down at the river ford
Beside the ferry,
Dances a little wherry,
To every wave that blows in from the sea
It dances merrily;
To every wave it dips it
And to the wind it tips it.
This merry little boat the king will take,
The pale queen waits with outstretched hands,
And now he bends above the oars,
And now before the garden gates he stands—
It was an eery thing to see
Him leave so merrily—
The music played him to the shore
Where he will walk no more.
The king is mad to be so lonely glad,
And mad to throw the key into the sea.

And now he dwells within his hermitage of bells
Upon the cape shaped like a hunter's horn,
The five bells strike a unitone,
The wind comes fooling like an ape
And the strange boy-breasted sea things mourn.
The rock pools seep and creep,
Laugh like a mad child in a moonstruck sleep,
And then flow onward like an easy dream,
Talking among the rocks,
Into one valley stream,

37

That ticks and drips and strikes like distant clocks
Till with a snaky motion
It curves three times
And glides into the ocean.
Marry! The king now is a lover!
The bridegroom of his mother earth, no other,
It goes unholily that he should be
Enamored of the earth that gave him birth
And of the sea,
But now he has his will
And he is husband to the sea and hill
And to the wind a brother.

At sunset all the garden swoons with bells,
Rolling across the sea and fells,
The demon sound stumbles along the ground,
Withering for miles around
And then is still—
All but one bell that dins on from the hill,
That strikes to ten,
While all the peasants pray
And cross themselves and say,
"Christ pity us!
It is the mad king's angelus,
Amen."

THE SEASONS.

WHEN Spring is born of Winter
    Then there comes a day
In early April with the warmth of May,
The clouds go gadding and the winds turn mild,
And Spring is born in sunlight,
Merry child!
Her nurse is April with the misty eyes;
The birds sing round her cradle
Where she lies
In green-streaked woodlands by the mantled ponds,
Where the young ferns unfurl their snaky fronds.

She comes up from the South
With a bird whistle on her pouting mouth,
And sits upon some hill
Her mother, Winter, has kept cold and still,
Till her Sun-lover melts the snow—
Then out the strong floods go,
Leaping like horses to the sea,
And the green frogs go mad with glee.
Ah! When that child is on her way
The trees make ready, in the North
The robins herald her
And the buds put forth.
Puss Willow's little catkins are a-stir,
And it is all, is all for her!

But for a little while
She lingers in the South,
Wandering the moss-draped aisle,
Brushing the shiest flowers with her mouth,
Tuning her swanny throat
To the lush warble of the swamp-bird's note,
Beneath the lamp-hung jasmine's vine tent
Her warm, delicious childhood soon is spent.

39

Then forth she fares,
About the middle of the month of May,
A young girl, wild-eyed, gay;
The mountains are her stairs,
The birds her harbingers,
With merry song
The peewit pipes her as she trips along—
The trumpet flowers blow fanfares.
Even the sea caves know her
And deep down
The mermen chime the bells
In some dim town,
Where wrecks lie rotten and forgotten;
The shark's fin glides
More avidly among the sea-isle tides—
The whole glad earth
Hails her with gales of mirth.
The frantic midges dance;
There is tumultuous lowing from the cattle.
When Spring fares northward from the South,
The young sun hungers for her cherry mouth
And the black stallions scream as if in battle.

SUMMER.

Now come the Dog Days
When the fat-faced sun
Like Falstaff pours hot jest
On Prince and thieves;
The earth at morning smokes
And at high noon
Straight downward point the listless hanging leaves.

Come, love, come, come away with me,
Beneath the arbor tree,
Where is sweet greenery and shade within;
Shall we not take our ease in love's own inn?

Come to that elfin place
Where fawns feed on the tender grass
And slim, shy shepherds come
To see their sunburnt face -
Upon a water glass,
Miraculously still—
Ah! Magic pool! They let the lead-sheep's bell
Grow fainter, fainter down the winding dell,
Until the only tone
That comes is the far *"lina-lina-lone"*
Of strayed sheep wandering on a windy hill.

Come, love, come, come away with me;
Drink from the coldest spring,
Where little frogs make Attic melody,
Tonight, perhaps, some moon-fooled bird will sing.

Dog Days,
I wish my love
Would come and live with me,
Beneath a tented tree,
The lush catalpa that in summer flowers,
Sol, I could laugh at thee!
If dalliance and sweet kisses sped the hours.

AUTUMN PORTENTS.

The amber foam creams from the cider flagons,
Backward the shadow of the ground-hog shrinks,
The lanes creak with the laden harvest wagons,
And the fur thickens on the owl-eyed lynx,
The hunter sees cold mist about the moon,
And in the bottom lands at morn,
The print of tiny, thievish, fairy hands
Where the raccoon last night went stealing corn.

AUTUMN INVOCATION.

"The seasons wait their turn among the stars."

Come from the blinding sun fields where you are,
Come from the interspace of star and star,
Summer lies sleeping in her dusty tomb,
The owlets mourn her through the woodland's gloom
Where all the night birds are.

Autumn, come down!

Into the columned forests cast your torches,
Light all their shadowed aisles like temple porches,
Stop at the Dog Star first and snatch his fire,
Bold sun-hot yellow and the red that scorches
To light dead summer's funeral pyre.

Autumn, come down!

Lean down, High Lady, from your starry arch,
Over the maples and the fragrant larch,
Stoop down some frosty night,
Like a proud maiden from an old, walled town
Tossing a rainbow favor to her knight.

Lean down, lean down!

Come take our northern forests for your palace,
Dance in the witch fires of the borealis,
Stand misty-eyed upon the mountain tops
Or sit and gaze,
With wind-twitched cloak and merry, cast-back hood,
Down valleys purpled by the grape-blue haze,
Beside some flaming wood.
Come throw your mad *flambeaux*
Till all the motley, fire-streaked woodlands glow!

Autumn, come down!

Lady, how often must I ask it?
Proud plenty, if you will, with vine-wreathed basket
Shall bring you offerings of damasked plums—
For you in orchards mellow peaches plash
All night.

The lichens whiten on the lonely ash,
The clover blackens and the last bee hums.

Autumn, come down,

You brown-skinned sorceress,
And witch the leaves, for harvest home,
And bear the nodding sheaves
Into the red barns by the little town,

Autumn, come down, come down!

DREAM FRAGMENT.

I WALKED last night in southern Brittany,
  In deep, warm meadows where the *rouge-gorge* sang,
A land cliff-bordered, by an azure sea,
Far off, far down, the muffled buoy bells rang
In bays that stretched into a land of indolence,
It seemed the peasants, in a fit of folly,
Had fled and left me in sweet impotence
To range blue uplands, tinged with melancholy,
In amethystine pastures, smooth and lone,
Charmed by a tepid ocean's magic moan.

WHEN SHADY AVENUE WAS SHADY LANE.

WHEN Shady avenue was Shady lane,
   Before the city fathers changed the name,
And cows stood switching flies beneath the trees,
And old-time gardens hummed with dusty bees,
And white ducks paddled in the summer rain;
Then everybody drove to church,
And Shady avenue was Shady lane.
We lived on Arabella street, that too
Is changed—Kentucky avenue—
And where the tollgate stood beside the spring,
The phlox and hollyhocks
Once flourished by the box
Where the gatekeeper sat with key and ring.
A wiser looking man there never was,
In contemplative mood he smoked and spat,
There by the gate he sat
In an old dog-eared hat
And listened to the yellow jackets' buzz.

All this is gone—
Gone glimmering down the ways
Of old, loved things of our lost yesterdays,
After the little tollgate by the spring.
And the gatekeeper odd
Rests in the quiet sod,
Safe in the arms of God
Where thrushes sing.
Even the spring has gone, for long ago
They walled that in,
And its dark waters flow
A sunless way along;
And no one stops to wonder where they go,
For no one hears their song.

Only a few old hearts
Of these much changed parts,
Whose time will soon run out on all the clocks,

Catching the scent of clover,
Live all the old days over
When Shady avenue was Shady lane.

Δ'S VERSUS ⊙'S.

Do you not see, you American people,
  What the triangle means?
Mind, soul, body.
Man is to live and die
In a little metaphysical, three-roomed apartment,
Office, chapel, and kitchenette.

As I sat and listened to the words of the wise man,
I looked out of the window
And suddenly a feeling of great well-being came on me.
I saw that I was made of the same stuff as the hillside
And that tomorrow I would be flowers,
Or dance in the dust motes in the sun
And that all things are one.

Then two laughing children came
And threw a stone into a fountain
And the ring widened till it was lost in the pool.
                    Behold a sign!
And I awoke and the wise man babbled like a fool.

And yet, O Great Republic,
The symbol of your state church
Is a triangle, blood red,
Pointing downward.

THE OLD JUDGE.

Around the courthouse corner from the square,
Where Poet Timrod's bust stands in the glare,
There is an ancient office shuttered tight,
With fluted pillars and the paint worn bare.
Seldom, if ever now, do passing feet
Disturb that little, cobbled *cul-de-sac*
Or rouse dull echoes in the quiet street
Where time has eddied back.
Only the old judge comes,
With quivering hands and thin,
With palsied scraping at the rusty lock
And enters in.
He is the last of all the courtly men,
Those lion-hearts who knew their Montesquieu,
And fought for what he taught them, too,
The STATE *was* something then—
But now—but now—he seems a very ghost
That haunts the little office off the square,
A Rip Van Winkle of the place at most
At which to stare.

Only on Saturdays he goes,
And no one knows,
And enters by the dusty, blinded door,
And sits and sits
While the long sunlight streams between the slits
And the rats scurry underneath the floor.
And there he stays all afternoon;
The wagons rumble in the square,
And the cracked, plaster bust of grim Calhoun
Frowns with its classic stare.
What dreams are these, old judge, of the old days,
When cotton bales made mountains on the ways,
When clipper ships were loading at the quays—
Or statelier, courtlier times of ease
And manners without flaw,
When *Smythe & Pringle,*

48

The name is all but weathered from the shingle,
Were the state's foremost firm at law.

Aye! Those *were* times!
They leap to life among the steeple chimes,
A passion and a white tone in the bells
Flatters his sleep until he dreams of bout
And rapier thrust at law—
Of frosty marches,
Camp fires and faces of dead men,
The War,
And old Virginia's academic arches—
And he is young again!
Oh! Life! Oh! Glory!
He leaps up from his seat—
Ah! Judge, the old, old story;
The blood can scarcely creep
Back to the icy feet
As the old man startles from his sleep,
The last bell hums and then—
Memento mori!

Dream, dream, old judge,
May quiet bring you ease,
Among the Wedgwood phantoms of old Greece,
Dream while the carved lambs in the frieze
Trot to the voiceless sound
Of Pan-pipes in the Georgian mantelpiece,
Summon the forms of men you used to know;
Till dead men's footfalls creak across the floor—
Is it your partner's who once long ago
Planted the brick court with *rêve d'or?*
Ah! He is gone now with his roses,
Gone these thirty years and more.

And now the new South quickens, in the square
The huge trucks thunder and the motors blare.
The park oaks droop with Spanish moss and age,
The *jedge* no longer now is *marss* but *boss,*

And all the old things suffer change and loss
But still he makes his weekly pilgrimage.
Some day, some waif will look in through the pane
And see him sitting with his gold-head cane
With wide unseeing eyes a-stare—
Then there will be an end of dreams and care,
A courtesy will pass we cannot spare,
And humor, sparkling, dry as old champagne.

BEWITCHED.

A LITTLE lad was he
Who loved a fisher maid in Brittany,
Where sands stretch flat and wide
When ebbs the tide,
Smooth as a threshing floor,
And there they played, young Véronique and Pierre,
Along the shore.
Often they used to walk
Hand fast in hand,
And laughed and kissed,
Lost in such heavenly talk
That spirits there,
Who dwelt in sunny places in the mist,
Drew very near to Véronique and Pierre,
And the shrill curlews cried,
And there were rainbow castles in the foam
Where seawites died.

Mornings, dear Véronique brought shells
And laid them on the stone beside Pierre's door,
Sea-shapes of beauty, magic as the stars,
Washed from old ocean's dragon-haunted floor,
And Pierre would dream that she was sitting there
And hoped that he would find her when he woke;
And so he did—and she would look at Pierre
And he at her—and neither of them spoke.
So passed July, whose molten hours flow,
The sun laughed hot and high,
And then they said good-bye,
For Pierre must go.
He left her standing dumbly in the lane,
Her lips a-tremble with his parting kiss,
And had her farewell gift, a twisted shell,
Bewitched! Bewitched! With melancholy spell,
For in that shell it was that little Pierre
First heard love's secret whispered thus, "De-ssspairr."

THE WINGLESS VICTORY.

NIKE of Samothrace,
    Thy godlike wings
Cleft windy space
Above the ships of kings,
Fain of thy lips,
By hope made glorious,
Time kissed thy grand, Greek face
Away from us.

Our Nike has no wings;
She has not known
Clean heights, and from her lips
Comes starvèd moan.
Mints lie that coin her grace,
And Time will hate her face,
For it has turned the world's hope
Into stone.

POEMS WRITTEN IN FRANCE AT THE FRONT
1918

THE BLINDMAN.

A BALLAD OF NOGENT L' ARTAUD.

AT Nogent, on the river Marne,
I passed a burning house and barn.
I went into the public square
Where pigeons fluttered in the air
And empty windows gaped a-stare.

There crouched a blindman by the wall
A-shivering in a ragged shawl,
Who gave a hopeless parrot screech
And felt the wall with halting reach.
He went around as in a trap.
He had a stick to feel and rap.
A-rap-a-tap, a-rap-a-tap.

I strode across the public square.
I stopped and spoke him full and fair.
I asked him what he searched for there.
There came a look upon his face
That made me want to leave the place.
He could not answer for a space.
He moved his trembling hands about
And in-and-out, and in-and-out.

"Kind sir," he said, "I scarcely know—
A week ago there fell a blow—
I think it was a week ago.
I sent my little girl to school,
With kisses and her book and rule,
A week ago she went to school."
The pigeons all began to coo,
"A-cock-a-loo, a-cock-a-loo."

"O God! to be a blinded fool;
I cannot find the children's school—
The gate, the court about the pool—
But, sir, if you will guide my feet

Across the square and down the street,
I think I know then where it lies.
O Jesu! Give me back my eyes!
O Jesu! Give me back my eyes!"

I led him down the littered street,
He seemed to know it with his feet,
For suddenly he turned aside
And entered through a gateway wide.
It was the court about the pool.
Long shadows slept there deep and cool.
No sound was there of beast or bird;
It was the silence that we heard.

"And this," he said, "might be the place,"
An eager look came on his face.
He raised his voice and gave a call;
An echo mewed along the wall,
And then it rose, and then it fell,
Like children talking down a well.
"Go in," he said, "see what you see,
And then come back again for me."

Like one who bears a weight of sin
And walks with fear, I entered in—
A turn—and halfway up the stair
There was a sight to raise your hair;
A dusty litter, books and toys,
Three bundles that were little boys,
White faces like an ivory gem;
A statue stood and looked at them.

So thick the silence where I stood,
I thought I wore a woolen hood;
The blood went whispering through my ears,
Like secrets that one overhears.
I looked upon the dead a while;
I saw the glimmering statue smile.
The children slept so sweetly there,
I scarce believed the tainted air.

And then I heard the blindman's stick,
As rhythmic as a watch's tick,
A step—a click, a step—a click—
As slow as days grow to a year,
So long it seemed while he drew near,
But sure and blind as death or fate,
He came and said, "I dared not wait.
It was too silent at the gate."

"And tell me now, sir, what you see
That keeps you here so silently."
"Three harmless things," I said, "I fear,
Three things I see but cannot hear,
Three shadows of what was before,
Cast by no light are on the floor."
"Sir," said the blindman, "lead me round,
Lest I should tread on holy ground."

Like men they lead at dawn to doom,
We slowly climbed the stairway's gloom
And came into a sunlit room.
The ceiling lay upon the floor,
And slates, and books, and something more—
The master with a glassy stare,
Sat gory in his shivered chair
And gazed upon his pupils there.

The blindman grasped me eagerly.
"And tell me now, sir, what you see?
This is the place where she should be—
My Eleanor, who used to wear
Short socks that left her brown legs bare.
She had a crown of golden hair."
I saw his blind eyes peer and stare.
Now there and here, now here and there.

"Blindman," I cried, "these things I see:
Time here has turned eternity.
The clock hands point but only mock,
For it is always three o'clock.

57

I see the shadows on the wall;
I see the crumbling plaster fall."
"Oh! sir," he said, "I crave your eyes—
Be not so kindly with your lies."

I drew the blindman to my side;
I told the truth I wished to hide.
I said, "I see your Eleanor
And she is dead upon the floor.
And something fumbles with her hair;
I guess the wind is playing there.
And I see gray rats sleek and stout
That dart about and dart about."

"Now, sir," he said, "I love your lies
And Christ be thanked that took my eyes!
But lead me, lead me to my dead!
And let me touch her once," he said.
I placed his hand upon her head.

And when we left the charnel place,
I dared not look upon his face;
For suddenly upon the street
Arose the sound of trampling feet,
And wheels that rumbled on the ground,
And ground around and ground around,
The din of them that go to slay,
The shout of men and horses' neigh,
And men and beasts swept on to war
A dreadful drumming on before.

It throbbed and throbbed through Nogent Town,
Till desolation settled down.
The blindman leaned against the door;
"And tell me, sir, about the war,
What is it they are fighting for?"
"Blindman," I cried, "Can you not see?
It is to set the whole world free!
It is for sweet democracy—"

"I do not know her, sir," he said.
"My little Eleanor is dead."

HANDS OFF.

DEDICATED TO ORATORS AND OTHERS.

I KNOW a glade in Argonne where they lean—
  Those crosses—loosened by last winter's snows,
Throwing their silent shadows on the green;
There I could go this very day—God knows!
To hide a sorrow mocked by tears and words,
To fall face downward on the catholic grass
That sprang this springtime through the shroud of snows
And let the little, greenwood birds say mass.

Like sound of taps at twilight from the hill,
The solemn thought comes that these lads are gone;
At evening when the breathing world grows still
And ghostly day steals from the bird-hushed lawn,
When over wooded crests the swimming moon
Casts ivory spells of beauty they have lost,
Across delicious valleys warm with June
I count the ghastly price the victory cost.

I count it in moongold and coin of life,
The love and beauty that these dead have missed,
Who lived to reap no glory from the strife,
But are like sleepers by the loved one kissed;
Each sleeps and knows not that she is so near,
Or at the most sinks deeper in his dream,
And life, and all blithe things they once held dear,
Are far and faint like voices of a stream.

Hands off our dead! For all they did forbear
To drag them from their graves to point some speech;
Less sickening was the gas reek over there,
Less deadly was the shrapnel's whirring screech;
You cannot guess the uttermost they gave;
Those martyrs did not die for chattering daws
To loot false inspiration from the grave
When mouthing fools turn ghouls to gain applause.

SOLDIER-POET.

To Francis Fowler Hogan.

I think at first like us he did not see
The goal to which the screaming eagles flew;
For romance lured him, France, and chivalry;
But Oh! Before the end he knew, he knew!
And gave his first full love to Liberty,
And met her face to face one lurid night
While the guns boomed their shuddering minstrelsy
And all the Argonne glowed with demon light.
And Liberty herself came through the wood,
And with her dear, boy lover kept the tryst;
Clasped in her grand, Greek arms he understood
Whose were the fatal lips that he had kissed—
Lips that the soul of Youth has loved from old—
Hot lips of Liberty that kiss men cold.

DOOMED.

Connigis from Bois de la Jutte, July, 1918.

Left to its fate, the little village stands
  Between the armies trenched on either hill,
Raising twin spires like supplicating hands
From meadow lands where all lies ghastly still.

The lakes of clover ripple to the breeze
As from the vineyards glides a rancid breath,
Bringing the homelike murmur of the bees,
Mixed with a sickening whiff of carrion death.

It is the valley of the shadow there,
Where death lies ambushed in the tossing flowers
Whose very beauty seems to cry, "*Beware!*"
For terror haunts its villages and towers.

That home where peasants led their blameless life,
That thatched, stone cottage is a clever trap
With painful wounds and fatal danger rife,
Noted with two red circles on the map.

Seen through the glass, dead, sleeps the *petite place*,
Where white-capped housewives lingered once to chat
On market days, or after early mass;
Now nothing moves there but the stealthy cat—

The only thing that even dares to stir;
It hugs short shadows near the walls at noon,
Lashing its tail to hear an airplane purr,
Circling about a peering, fat balloon.

The houses gleam too bright, their limelight glare,
Pure sunlight though it be, is filled with gloom;
They are too white, too garnished and too bare—
They are too much like walls about a tomb.

The windows stare beside each gaping door,
Where once in gingham apron and a shawl,
In days now passed away forevermore,
Some little mother sat and nursed her doll.

Sepulchral silence and a lonely dread
And desolation's calm have settled down,
Making brief peace there for the rigid dead—
Tonight the shells will burst upon the town!

WHITE LIGHT.

How like high mountain air this air in France;
The sun is so intense, so clear, so bright,
The fields unearthly green, the poplars glance,
Shivering their leafy lances in the light.
Those drilling troops flash back a steely gleam.
Others with distant din of clean delight,
Bathe where their bodies flash along the stream
And everywhere, the air, a lake of light!

White light, strange light of tense romantic days,
You are too rare, too cloudless and too clear,
Like a deep crystal where a seer might gaze
And see some vast disaster drawing near.

Petite Villiers,
July 4th, 1918.

BEAUMONT.

DEEP in the mystery of the woodland's gloom,
   Topping the sea of trees with pointed cone,
So that from many hills its towers loom,
The old château of Beaumont stands alone.
This generation saw its last sons go
To spill their noble blood with humbler men;
So Madame lives alone at the château
And waits for steps that never come again.
The sunlight sleeps along the buttressed walls,
And on the stagnant moats the midges dance,
And in the haunted wood the cuckoo calls,
Where hunted once the vanished kings of France.
The terraced gardens hum with greedy bees,
And Madame walks among the orange trees.

Boxed orange shrubs—they stand in potted row
Along the plaisance—Madame takes her ease;
But it is lonely at the old château;
The milky statues glimmer through the trees,
So silent, too! What can make Madame start?
Down in the garden where late roses blow,
She has heard laughter there that stopt her heart
Like echoes from old summers long ago.
But no—it cannot be! For hark! the click
Of little peasants' sabots; down the walk
That winds among the rows of hedges thick,
The children's voices die away in talk.
Alas! Who knows, who knows,
Why Madame bends so long above the rose?

Gently, old heart—there is no recompense
For the last uttermost you had to give.
Yet there is peace for you to outward sense—
God gives you Beaumont as a place to live.
The white herds graze in stately indolence,
While you sit knitting on the terrace there,
And that your hands still feel no impotence,
Witness the poor and *Croix Rouge* at St. Pierre;

And sweet the drive home through the wooded park,
When faintly chime the far-off steeple clocks
At dusk when village dogs begin to bark,
And the long lanes go glimmering white with flocks,
When the first, steely stars begin to peep
And the young shepherd whistles to his sheep.

St. Pierre-Le Moutier,
1918.

VILLIERS LE BEL GONNESSE.

HERE in this garden where the roses bloom,
   And time is scarcely marked by silent days,
The walls and pear trees cast a pleasant gloom,
A wavy, weed-grown fountain softly plays.
And fate has left us listless for a while
Upon the brink of what we do not know;
Outside the walls a passing schoolboy calls,
And lumbering oxcarts rumble as they go.

Red roofs, a spire, white roads and poplar trees;
An aeroplane goes droning through the skies;
The petals fall, there is no breath of breeze;
The old dog by the sundial snaps at flies.
My comrades by the fountain are asleep.
Far on the lines I hear a great gun boom;
Here in the garden, though, white peace lies deep,
And in the limelight heat the roses bloom.

DRAGON'S BREATH.

WE held the last stone wall—when day was red—
    They crept like morning shadows through the dead,
The *flammenwerfer* with their dragon's breath
Compressed in nippled bottle-tanks of death.

They puffed along the wall and one long cry
Withered away into the morning sky,
And some made crablike gestures where they lay
And all our faces turned oil gray,
Before the smoke rolled by.

It is beyond belief
How men can live
All curled up like a leaf.

I saw a man bloom in a flower of flame,
Roaring with fire,
Three times he called a name;
Three times he whirled within a white-hot pod
With busy hands and cried, "Oh, God! Oh, God!"

Now when the trumpets lie with blusterous joy
And the silk, wind-tweaked colors virgin fresh,
Borne by the blithe, boy bodies glitter past,
As the old gladiators throw their mesh;
The dragon's breath leaps from the bugle blast
And Azrael comes pounding with his drum—
Fe, fe, . . . fi, fo, fum—
I smell the roasting flesh!

WE.

WE who have come back from the war,
    And stand upright and draw full breath,
Seek boldly what life holds in store
And eat its whole fruit rind and core,
Before we enter through the door
To keep our rendezvous with death.

We who have walked with death in France,
When all the world with death was rife,
Who came through all that devils' dance,
When life was but a circumstance,
A sniper's whim, a bullet's glance,
We have a rendezvous with life!

With life that hurtles like a spark
From stricken steel where anvils chime,
That leaps the space from dark to dark,
A blinding, blazing, flaming arc,
As clean as fire, and frank and stark—
White life that lives while there is time.

We will not live by musty creeds,
Who learned the truth through love and war,
Who tipped the scales for right by deeds,
When old men's lies were broken reeds,
We follow where the cold fact leads
And bow our heads no more.

Deliver us from tactless kin,
And drooling bores that start "reforms,"
And unctious folk that prate of sin,
And theorists without a chin,
And politicians out to win,
And generals in uniforms.

We have come back who broke the line
The hard Hun held by bomb and knife!
All but the blind can read the sign;

The time is ours by right divine,
Who drank with Death in blood red wine,
We have a rendezvous with life!

ND - #0051 - 160323 - C0 - 229/152/4 [6] - CB - 9780331009774 - Gloss Lamination